SHE THINKS LIKE A LEADER

BUSINESS AFFIRMATIONS

JEMMA ROEDEL

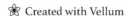 Created with Vellum

We hope these affirmations bring you all the success you deserve!

∼

Join our community on Facebook for daily business advice and a great support network of business women She Thinks Like a Boss

∼

Find us on instagram for weekly quotes and inspiration
www.instagram.com/shethinkslikeaboss

Introduction

YOU MIGHT BE WONDERING what affirmations are, how they work and why they are good for you. Affirmations are positive statements that help you to tackle any negative thinking patterns you may have developed over time. When used correctly, affirmations will remove all of your negative thoughts and replace them with positive thoughts.

WORDS ARE AN EXTREMELY POWERFUL TOOL. When affirmations are spoken out loud regularly, they have the power to not only transform your thoughts, but also your behaviour and emotions. They can also be used to inspire and influence other people as well, making them the ideal resource for anyone who runs a business or is looking to run a business in the future.

OF COURSE, when put into practice, affirmations can help you achieve your individual goals, but they can also help bring a team of people together to achieve collective goals. For daily inspiration and affirmations that will help you make improvements in all areas of your business, you should join **She Thinks Like A Boss** – a Facebook community group aimed at women in business.

. . .

AFFIRMATIONS HAVE HELPED millions of people from all over the world create positive changes in their lives. However, there are many people who are sceptical about whether affirmations actually work. But what have you got to lose? Nothing negative ever came from using affirmations, so you may as well just bite the bullet and give it a go.

BY USING AFFIRMATIONS, you'll regularly remind yourself of your goals, which in turn will encourage you to take action towards achieving them. Instead of thinking negatively throughout your day, daily affirmations will reprogram your brain to only think positive thoughts. Talking about yourself in a positive light will install new beliefs into your subconscious mind as well as boost your self-confidence and make you feel good about yourself.

BUT REMEMBER IT IS A PRACTICE, something you need to engage with on a regular basis, preferably every day, maybe even twice per day. Doing affirmations once per week or once per month won't give you enough concentrated time to alter and reprogram the negative patterns you've developed over the years.

FOR THOSE WHO are not familiar with using affirmations you can begin your journey by choosing a selection from the list we've provided. To start, pick out between 5 and 10 sentences that resonate with you, or express something you would like to achieve in your life or want to believe about yourself. As time goes on you can add as many to your list as you like. Also feel free to adapt them slightly to fit your own personal needs, or you could even try writing some of your own.

. . .

ONCE YOU'VE CHOSEN some affirmations, write them down on a piece of paper and put them in a place that you're guaranteed to look every morning. This could be your bathroom mirror, your refrigerator or somewhere near your kettle (everyone loves a morning cup of coffee right?).

WHEN YOU WAKE UP, as soon as you see your list, give yourself some time to speak your affirmations out loud. It doesn't have to take too long, even if you can only dedicate 5 minutes to your list, this will still make a big difference.

YOU CAN SPEAK your affirmations out loud as many times as you like until you're really focussing on the thought and the feeling. This means you will always begin your day by doing something positive. By starting your day on a positive note, you'll have a better chance of continuing your day this way.

YOU SHOULD ALSO SPEAK your affirmations out loud again before you go to bed. Some people believe that doing affirmations before you sleep, as well as hearing them out loud whilst you sleep, is more effective than at any other time of the day. The reason for this is because when you're falling asleep your body enters a theta brain state. A theta brain state is when your body releases a chemical that slows down your brain activity and puts you in a sort of hypnotic state (somewhere between being awake and asleep). This puts you in the perfect position to start to subconsciously absorb your affirmations.

YOU WILL THEN ENTER a delta brain state. This is when you are completely asleep. When you are fully asleep your conscious mind is no longer blocking thoughts from going to your subconscious mind, which leaves your subconscious mind more open to receiving and absorbing.

TRY and do your affirmations every single day, morning and evening if you can. But please don't worry too much if you ever miss them. Affirmations are there to make you feel good, if you're stressing about them then you're completely missing the point.

1

I am the master of my visions and the universe admires my brilliance. I let go of all resistance and I am ready to fulfil my ambitions.

2

I adore my quirks because they make me unique.

❧

I am powerful and I am running my business with maximum energy and enthusiasm.

❧

3

I am naturally talented and my business is reaching maximum heights.

I am the master of my destiny and I am creating a wonderful life through the use of my mind and energy.

4

I love abundance and prosperity.

～

I am in control of my mind, body and soul.

～

5

The universe has my back and I achieve success in everything I put my mind to. I am powerful.

~

The universe is within me and I am growing positively everyday.

~

6

I am the master of my life and my business is a huge success.

∽

Prosperity and abundance is my birth right and I shall have it. My life is amazing just the way it is.

∽

7

I am in love with myself and my life.

∼

I enjoy being the boss of my own business and turning it into my own empire.

∼

8

～

I am confident and worthy enough to attract wonderful opportunities and amazing clients who will work their best for me.

～

I forgive myself for all the mistakes I have made and will learn from them.

～

9

I am so much more than I thought I could be, I am amazing just the way I am.

I am worthy of all the greatness the world has to offer me and I am very grateful for everything I have already received.

10

My energy is infinite and I am fueled by confidence, faith and optimism.

~

I am capable of achieving every dream and every desire I have, I will achieve it with my limitless power.

~

11

I am a force which attracts only positivity and great miracles in life. I am worthy of all the great things I attract.

I am the queen of my business and I am increasing my profits every day using my brilliant mind.

12

I am gorgeous and amazing with a unique spirit. I am a winner.

I am unstoppable and will take things to the next level and achieve massive success.

13

I am infinitely powerful and the conqueror of all abundance and wealth.

I am a high-spirited person and my actions make a difference in my work and activities.

14

I believe in myself wholeheartedly and I am the master of my life, attracting all the greatness I deserve.

I am fearless like a lioness, I will achieve massive success and happiness for I deserve the best in the world.

15

My body, mind and spirit are within my control. I create positive vibrations to attract massive success in whatever I put my heart into. My energy is limitless.

I release all the blocks attracting money, and wealth flows effortlessly and naturally to me.

16

I am smart, I am loved, I am amazing, I am gorgeous and I am enough.

I deeply, completely accept myself and I am very proud of myself. I am the source of the universe. My energy is limitless.

17

My life is bursting with love, happiness and prosperity.

I am unstoppable in achieving my goals.

18

I choose to be calm and peaceful and the world is a better place because I am here today.

~

I release all doubts and insecurities. I am open to all the new opportunities life has laid out before me.

~

19

I am open to becoming my highest self and I manifest all of my dreams with my infinite power.

Wealth, happiness and abundance surrounds me, and my business is number one on the market.

20

My business empire is at its best and is growing every day.

～

I am grateful for everything I have in my life, everything I desire is already within me and I can manifest it with great ease.

～

21

My thoughts create my reality and nothing is impossible in my life.

∼

I release all negative emotions and thoughts regarding money and I am open to receiving abundance and prosperity.

∼

22

My entire focus is on positive thoughts and I reject and block any negativity in my life.

23

I allow myself to overcome all negative thoughts and limiting beliefs and I am replacing them with positive thoughts and vibrations.

24

I am worthy, I am deserving and I am the queen. I am more than enough.

25

God is continuously protecting me and I am very thankful for all the abundance he is giving me.

26

The business mindset I have is excellent, I am the attractor of many amazing clients and opportunities.

27

I am inspiring and magical being with infinite energy.

28

Fear and anxiety cannot control my life. I am the ruler of my life and I rule it efficiently and effectively.

29

I uphold the standards I have for myself. I deserve it and I am a pro manifestor.

30

I am proud of my decisions and I know good things are continuously happening in my life.

31

The universe has my back. I am completely fearless of all the challenges life has for me.

32

I am succeeding in my career even if I am not yet where I want to be in life.

33

I am celebrating my small wins whilst keeping my eye on the end goal.

34

I may have bad days, but the sun will shine again. I trust in miracles and myself.

35

I have a truly positive attitude towards money and I am really thankful for all the wealth I currently have in my life.

36

My business is growing at a huge rate and I am set to be number one in the world. I am worthy and deserving of it.

37

I am worthy of receiving income and I release all negative financial energy.

～

I am a success magnet and I believe that clients come to me easily.

～

38

Good things keep coming to me. I have a wonderful business with a wonderful income and I am very grateful for it.

I will become the first millionaire in my family and I am completely capable of achieving greatness.

39

I am creating the life of my dreams and everything is always working for me.

I am keeping my body healthy, my mind strong, and my soul tranquil to attract all the goodness that is in store for me.

40

Failing only brings me closer to greatness and I am achieving everything I put my mind to.

～

My unique talents and skills can make a profound difference in this world and I am destined to do great things.

～

41

I respect money, I love money, I attract money and I have money.

～

I embrace the rhythm of life and I let it unfold in beautiful ways.

～

42

I am aware that my intuition will always guide me towards my best and I'm very proud of it.

~

I am a high achiever and I reach my goals very easily. Success flows naturally to me.

~

43

I am in charge of my happiness and I am 100% responsible for my own life.

I welcome every day with a new fresh energy and I am living a happy, satisfied, peaceful life.

44

Changing my mindset for good is my strength and I adore my strengths and weaknesses.

~

Every part of me is unique and I'm very happy with it.

~

45

I have all that I need to make today a great day.

My life is a masterpiece that I am creating. I am a beautiful work of art with infinite abilities.

46

I am healthy, energetic and unwaveringly optimistic.

I am conscious of everything around me and my heart is completely open to greatness.

47

I am aware that I am worth a thousand millions. I have an amazing mind and personality.

≈

The universe is filled with innumerable possibilities for my business.

≈

48

My business is unique, will conquer the world and have massive success.

As life brings new challenges, I am becoming more confident, brave and powerful.

49

I'm uncontrollable with limitless energy and no one can stop me from achieving what I deserve.

∾

I am my own superhero and I believe in the power of manifestation.

∾

50

I forgive those who have harmed me in the past and I peacefully detach myself from them.

∼

Today I abandon my old habits and invite new ones.

∼

51

I am the architect of my own life and I am creating my life perfectly. .

I believe in the power of giving and I believe that whatever I give comes back to me.

52

I am letting go of attachments to outcome and I am completely filled with positive energy.

I emit positive vibrations which brings huge success and prosperity into my life.

53

I will never let a situation or another person affect my well-being.

～

People look up to me and I inspire them with my actions and words.

～

54

My body and mind is healing by the mercy of God and the universe.

I am the all-knowing universe and have the ability to create anything and everything I desire.

55

My business is inspiring and is winning the hearts of many people.

I am blessed to be living in this modern era where everything I desire is right at my fingertips. I feel powerful today.

56

I am giving my complete focus and attention to what I do without worrying about the outcome. I know the fruits of my actions are always amazing.

I am enjoying life to the fullest and I love life for everything it has given me.

57

I am a born leader and I am not worried about other people's opinion of me.

~

I love myself. My body and my mind deserve my absolute care and attention.

~

58

In my life there is no such thing as a wrong decision.

~

I'm free of worries and at absolute peace with who I am.

~

59

I can and I will.

I am breathing in courage and exhaling doubts and insecurities as
they no longer serve me or my purpose.

60

I am self-aware and I know what's best for me and my life.

I have the power to create change and I do it with no regrets as I am the queen.

61

While I'm happy I think because I know my happy thoughts are becoming my reality.

～

Nothing is impossible, the word itself says I'm possible.

～

62

I manage my own life and I am making it a huge success.

~

I'm flawed but these flaws make me beautiful and unique.

~

63

Today is my day and I'm gonna conquer everything I desire.

I am open to great peace, great joy and great love.

64

I am excited about life and I'm living in complete bliss.

I am going to achieve great things today as I'm fully energized by the passion inside of me.

65

I am alive so everything is ok. Where there is life there is hope.

I am a masterpiece created by God and I am totally aware of my potential.

66

I am a phenomenal personality with all the powers needed to
conquer everything I desire.

～

I am daring like a lioness. I am going to live every moment and never
regret it.

～

67

The sky is the limit. I am the universe and I am capable of anything
and everything.

I listen to my body's needs. I'm very grateful for the body I live in and
I'm nourishing it with love.

68

I listen to my thoughts and through using mindfulness I let go of anything negative.

~

To receive love and affection I know I have to give love and affection. I receive what I give.

~

69

I am totally conscious of myself and I am provided for from the outside world.

I am completely content within myself.

70

I am the reason for my joy, well-being and wealth. I love myself.

Every single cell in my body is filled with happiness, wealth and vitality.

71

I am the attractor of positive clients and opportunities which is bringing my business to its peak.

Every small action I'm taking today will have incredible results in the future.

72

I quit living in the past and worrying about the future, instead I choose to blissfully live in the present.

I believe in myself and every action I take is boosting my business to great heights.

73

I am thrilled and excited about the person I'm becoming. The process is amazing and is bringing me closer to the universe.

I am constantly energized by my passion and I honour my commitments and promises.

74

I am growing through every experience and I'm very much determined to succeed.

~

I am nature, so I respect nature and respect myself for I hold the same qualities as mother nature

~

75

I am being patient and focussing on my work rather than the outcomes.

I am waking up today filled with confidence, happiness and empowerment.

76

I am stronger with every step I take and my experiences make me who I am.

Today I am embracing simplicity, peace and solace because I value its importance in life.

77

I'm blessed beyond measure. I'm dependable and resourceful.

≈

I'm talented and radiate positivity and confidence.

≈

78

I'm loved and I love everyone as what I give is what I receive.

~

My income is constantly increasing and I'm wealthy beyond my wildest dreams.

~

79

I have beautiful and unique qualities to offer this world.

By becoming the best version of myself I can positively impact the world.

80

I am one of a kind and I unconditionally accept myself the way I am.

All of my businesses are experiencing huge successes and I'm very thankful for everything I have in my life.

81

I won't apologize for being me, I am worthy of all the goodness.

All is well in my world and I choose to be grateful for everything I have.

82

I love my body and mind for all it does for me.

I am attracting the most beautiful energies from where I am at this
very moment.

83

I'm unaffected by the judgement of others, I am worthy of being a leader.

I choose to be amazing when everyone is trying hard to be normal.

84

I let go of all that is out of my control and focus on the things that are within my control.

Nothing can stop me from leading life on my own terms and I choose remain peaceful.

85

Everything is working out well and the universe is always working behind the scenes for my ultimate good.

I am prepared to take advantage of every opportunity life has given me.

86

I am never a failure, I either win or I learn, therefore I am always a winner.

The empire I run is absolutely amazing and has a positive energy and wonderful clients.

87

I am strong and powerful and I am ruling my empire with knowledge and passion.

I believe in myself enormously.

88

I am always there for myself and I don't have to fear anything in this world.

～

The world is full of miracles and I am one of them. I am beautiful, intelligent and thriving.

～

89

My happiness is what matters most to me. As long as I am happy, I don't care what others think.

I love my uniqueness. My skills are impressing people in many different ways.

90

I am courageous and I can get through whatever life throws at me.

∼

I am happy and free because I am me.

∼

91

My life is a blast of growing opportunities because I never fail to create them.

I am a powerful woman who is surrounded by success and happiness.

92

I work well under pressure and I am always motivated.

∼

There is a strong force in me that fights against all negativity and evil.

∼

93

I am very optimistic in life and failures are part of my journey.

I handle failures with great ease. Failure is the stepping stone to success.

94

In a way I am uncontrollable, no one can control me except myself.

～

The devil works hard but I work harder.

～

95

I am capable of everything and will never give up.

∾

Creativity and talent are my gifts.

∾

96

I am fulfilled and content with who I am and what I have. I am independent.

I will never surrender to failure.

97

Victory in my job and life is making me a woman of many wonderful qualities.

I adore myself and the people around me. My life is filled with love and mercy.

98

My positive emotions attract positive things in my life which is what makes me so successful.

～

I have everything I need to overcome every obstacle in life.

～

99

I'm in control of my mind, body and soul and I'm managing them with great ease.

I am a powerful ruler with great skills and all of my enemies will be easily defeated.

100

I am capable of solving all of my problems in my own way.

I trust the universe and always let go of any obsession over outcomes.
I have the most powerful abilities within me.

101

Whatever I've always wanted is already within me and will soon be manifested.

My life is bursting with energy and I always believe in the power within me.

102

My body is healthy, my mind Is brilliant and my soul is tranquil.
Everything is working for me.

I am the greatest warrior I have ever seen and I am continuously
fighting for all my dreams to come true.

103

My ability to negotiate and handle my business is perfect, I am no less than a super woman.

Today, I am going to have the best day and I am going to complete all of my tasks with ease.

104

I am effortlessly manifesting everything I have always wished for.

I am a powerful woman. I am the greatest and I trust myself.

105

I don't fear insecurities, insecurities fear me.

I am strong and never surrender to the dramas of life.

106

I am going to make a positive impact on the world.

I am liberating myself with the knowledge of the universe and this is making me a smarter and more peaceful being than ever before.

107

I am investing my young, spirited energy into making a huge impact on the world.

I am capable of making changes and I AM THE CHANGE.

108

I am attracting magic from the universe into my life because being joyful is my priority.

I am totally in control of my life and I am the master of everything I do.

109

I am leading a very positive life full of magic and great success.

I am the creator of my destiny and I have already mastered this art.

110

Every part of my life is in my hands and I will never compromise.

I am healthy, strong, optimistic and joyful.

111

I enjoy coming to work every day as it is my own empire and I am the boss.

I forgive myself for all the mistakes I have made. I am enough and my abilities are amazing.

112

I am so much more than what I thought I could be. I am amazing just the way I am.

I am capable of every dream and desire I have and I will achieve them with my limitless power

113

I am a force which attracts only positivity and great miracles and I am worthy of it.

I am filled with calm energy knowing the universe has my back. I am tranquil and peaceful.

114

I am ready to allow miracles to flow into my life.

∼

I am getting stronger every day. If I ever feel in danger, I know it's just my mind playing tricks on me.

∼

115

I am getting rich doing what I love and with my passion I will keep
the fire constantly burning.

I am a powerful creator.

116

I am happy to give my money as I know every penny I give always comes back to me.

My business is reaching maximum heights and I am adored by many.

117

I am the creator of my wealth and I am living abundantly.

I am blessed by the almighty in heaven as I'm smart, beautiful and purehearted.

118

I am tuned into the flow of prosperity. I dream, I believe and I receive.

I trust the universe with everything it has got in store for me. I am healthy, wealthy and happy.

119

I am focusing on my positive thoughts of being financially secure. I am grateful for all the money that I currently have.

I am improving daily and my progress is continuous.

120

I control of all my actions and thoughts and I am aware that the future has amazing things in store for me.

My business is reaching its highest potential and is effortlessly attracting clients and income.

121

I am getting stronger every day and becoming more connected to my true inner self.

I am constantly discovering new sources of income and I release all negative energy associated with finances.

122

I let go of all negativity, leaving egotistical and selfish behaviors behind.

I am realistic with my dreams and know that I am the greatest of all time.

123

I have great power within me. I work and hold conversations with amazing confidence and personality.

I shine like a bright night star amidst the darkness of this world.

124

I glow and shine like a bright star with a charming personality.

I trust my journey and know that I abundance follows me everywhere I go.

125

My mind is full of brilliant ideas and my body is healthy. I am totally in love with myself.

I embrace my uniqueness. I am living a blessed and miraculous life.

126

Everything I touch turns into gold. I am the master of abundance.

~

I am a powerful woman who can change the world.

~

127

I am happy that my dreams are slowly turning into reality and that I am receiving everything I deserve.

I am grateful for every second of my life and all of the wonderful opportunities to discover amazing things. The future is an exciting mystery.

128

Today is a new day full of surprises and possibilities and I am creating the best version of my life.

Happiness flows to me like a flowing river and I am realizing that everything I want has always been within me.

129

I am living a great life. I believe in myself and I am open to receiving everything I deserve.

I am a wonderful creator and I am creating the life of my dreams.

130

My powerful spirit is attracting great miracles, paving the way for abundance.

The universe supports me in every way and I am extremely grateful for all of the love and support.

131

All is well in my world. I am feeling safe and peaceful and everything is working out the way I want it to.

The universe is working behind the scenes, but even though I can't see it, I still believe in its magic.

132

I am extremely lucky and am constantly receiving amazing opportunities.

I am fit and well. I have a healthy body and I'm living a wealthy life.

133

I am financially free and positivity fills my life.

∾

Everything is working out for the best. I trust the process and believe I am worthy of greatness.

∾

134

I have the power within me to solve any challenges that come my way.

I am a woman with spirit and and my mind is damn powerful.

135

I am a boss who manages her empire with great ease.

I let go of any negativity through mindfulness and living in the present.

136

The world needs me and I am always grateful for this.

I am conscious of myself and I am content within myself.

137

Abundance, wealth and prosperity flows through every cell of my body.

I believe in myself fully and I love myself unconditionally..

138

I am fit, gorgeous and intelligent.

≈

Finally, I am myself, I love myself and I am proud to be me.
--------------------♥--------------------

FINAL WORDS

NO DOUBT JUST HEARING THESE affirmations read aloud has already put you in a better, more positive and productive state of mind. Creating a successful business can be tough at times, so that's why it's important to put yourself in the best position possible to succeed.

IF YOU'RE FEELING a little unsure about the affirmations process and you're worried you're going to end up wasting your time, feel free to give yourself a cut off point. Tell yourself that you will give affirmations your all for one month and if nothing has changed by the end of the month you are going to quit. I guarantee that you will get to the end of that month and want to continue.

AFTER A MONTH OF DOING AFFIRMATIONS, you will be feeling happier, stronger, more positive, more grateful, more in control, more successful and more at peace.

. . .

WHETHER YOU'RE JUST STARTING out in business, or you've been running a business for a long time, mindset is the key. Having a positive outlook is integral to your success. Having a negative outlook will only sabotage your success. If you let thoughts creep in such as "I'm a failure" or "I'm not good enough" then you're more likely to fail and this will result in you feeling not good enough. But if you tell yourself that you're successful and that you are good enough (and most importantly you believe it) you're much more likely to succeed.

ONE OF THE most beneficial things you can do is learn to be happy in the present moment. Get rid of that internal narrative that convinces you that you can only be happy once your business earns a certain amount of profit, or you can only be happy once you've hired a certain amount of staff, or you can only be happy once you're recognized as successful by other businesses within your field.

WITH THIS KIND OF MINDSET, you will never be happy because once you achieve these things, you will inevitably want more. The narrative will then change to fit your new aspirations and you'll only be able to be happy once you've achieved these new goals. If you choose to be happy in the here and now, everything else will automatically fall into place.

ALONGSIDE YOUR AFFIRMATIONS, surround yourself with positive reinforcement. Stick your most inspiring quotes up around your office and at home, only follow positive social media accounts and surround yourself with people who make you feel good. One of the toughest things to do in life is to cut people out who bring you nothing but negativity. This could be colleagues, friends or sometimes even family. If it's too difficult to cut them out of your life completely, you should consider minimizing your time with them.

Once you surround yourself with nothing but positivity you will begin to notice everything falling into place effortlessly and you'll wonder why you didn't start this journey sooner.

Take the next important step in your journey by following **She Thinks Like a Boss** on Facebook and Instagram to become part of a community filled with strong businesswomen, like yourself. Here you will be welcomed by a friendly and supportive network of incredible women and will be gifted with daily inspirational and motivational business advice.

Find us on instagram for weekly quotes and inspiration
www.instagram.com/shethinkslikeaboss

Facebook Group
She Thinks Like a Boss : A Community for Business Women

Thank You

Made in United States
Orlando, FL
03 October 2024

52125500R00083